Time to Sign

SIGN LANGUAGE FOR KIDS

by Kathryn Clay

illustrated by

Michael Reid, Randy Chewning,

Margeaux Lucas, and Daniel Griffo

CAPSTONE PRESS
a capstone imprint

TABLE OF CONTENTS

Brief Introduction to American Sign Language (ASL)

Many people who are deaf or hard of hearing use ASL to talk. Hearing people may also learn ASL to communicate with deaf friends and family members.

Signs can be very different from one another. Signs may use one or both hands. Sometimes signs have more than one step. For other signs, you must move your entire body. If there is no sign for a word, you can fingerspell it.

People use facial expressions when they sign. They smile when signing good news. They frown when signing sad news. Body language is also important. Someone might sign slowly to show that he or she is very tired.

It's important to remember that learning to sign is like learning any language. ASL becomes easier with practice and patience.

How to Use This Guide

This book is full of useful words in both English and American Sign Language (ASL). The English word and sign for each word appear next to the picture. Arrows are used to show movement for some signs.

Most ASL signs are understood wherever you go. But some signs may change depending on where you are. It's like having a different accent.

For example, New Yorkers sign "pizza" like this:

People in other places might sign "pizza" like this:

or this:

People will not understand you if they can't see your signs. Make sure your hands are always in view when signing with someone. Don't be afraid to ask people to slow down or sign again if you don't understand a sign.

ALPHABET CHART

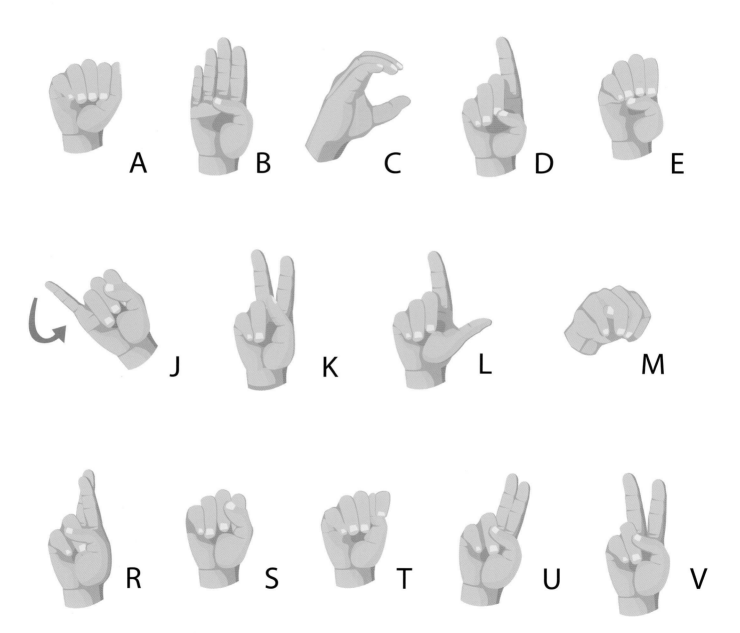

ASL has a sign for every letter of the English alphabet. If there is no sign for a word, you can use letter signs to spell out the word. Fingerspelling is often used to sign the names of people and places.

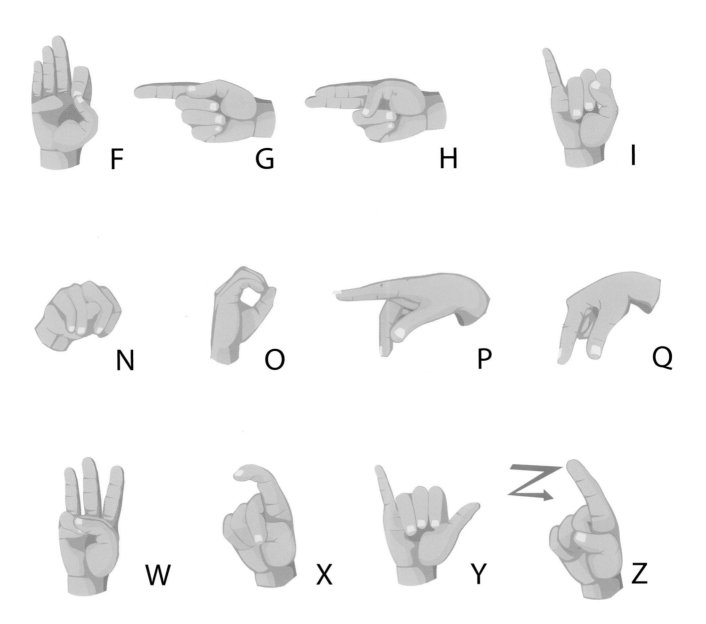

F   G   H   I

N   O   P   Q

W   X   Y   Z

BODY

Slide hands down chest.

eyes Point to each eye.

head Bring hand to chin.

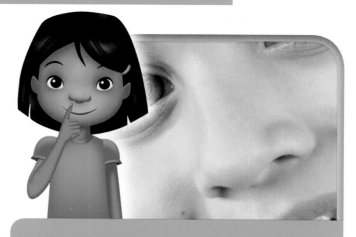

nose Tap nose twice.

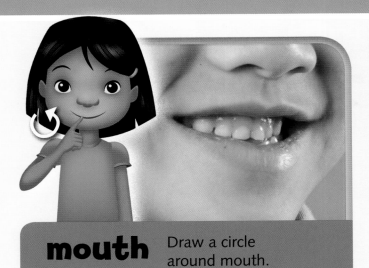

mouth Draw a circle around mouth.

arm Slide hand down arm.

hand Slide palm over bottom hand.

leg Point to leg.

foot Point to foot.

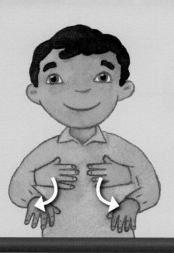

CLOTHES

Slide hands down and out.

pants Bring hands up twice.

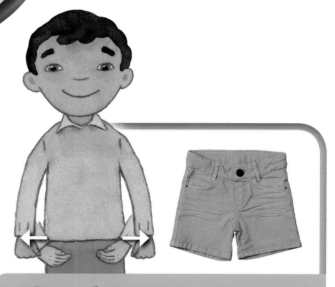

shorts Slide hands to sides.

socks Rub fingers together.

shoes   Bring fists together.

hat   Pat head twice.

pajamas
1. Close hand in front of face.
2. Slide hands down and out.

shirt   Grab shirt and pull.

coat   Bring fists together.

TOYS

Fingerspell T-O-Y-S.

ball   Bring fingers together.

train   Slide fingers back and forth.

puzzle   Lock fingers together.

doll   Slide finger down nose.

board game
1. Slide hands to sides.
2. Make A shapes and tap knuckles together twice.

FAMILY

Make F shapes and move hands in a circle.

baby Rock arms back and forth.

mother Touch thumb to chin. **father** Touch thumb to forehead.

brother
1. Place thumb on forehead.
2. Bring wrists together.

sister
1. Slide thumb along cheek.
2. Bring wrists together.

grandfather
1. Make the sign for "father."
2. Bounce hand away from forehead.

grandmother
1. Make the sign for "mother."
2. Bounce hand away from chin.

uncle Move U shape in a circle.

aunt Move A shape in a circle.

cousin Shake C shape by side of head.

PETS

Rub hand twice.

dog Pat leg. Snap fingers.

cat Pretend to pull whiskers on face.

bird Open and close fingers.

mouse Brush finger across nose.

snake Bend fingers and slide back and forth.

turtle Stick out thumb. Cover hand and wiggle thumb.

rabbit Cross hands. Move fingers up and down.

fish Hold hand sideways and wiggle.

FEELINGS

Move middle finger up chest.

sad Move hands down in front of face.

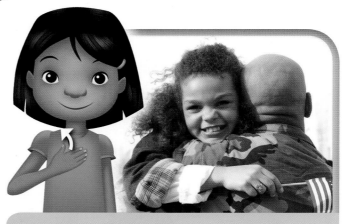

happy Make two small circles at chest.

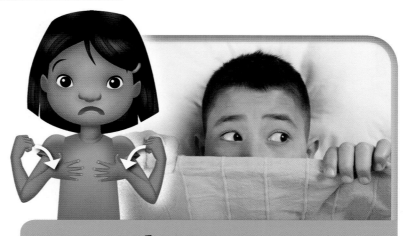

scared
1. Make fists.
2. Open hands with palms facing chest.

18

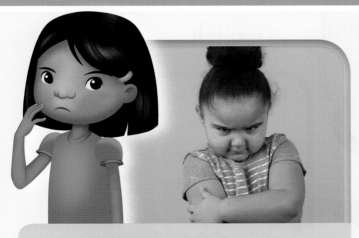

angry Bend fingers and bring toward face.

surprised Make fists and point index fingers.

excited
1. Bend middle fingers.
2. Make small circles at chest.

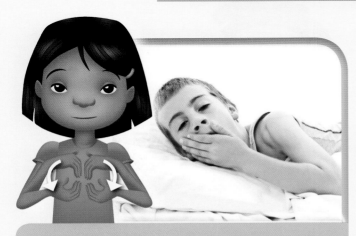

tired Bend wrists down.

bored Twist finger at side of nose.

SPORTS

Move thumbs back and forth.

football Lace fingers together twice.

baseball Move hands like swinging a bat.

hockey Curl finger and slide along palm.

basketball — Move wrists forward twice.

soccer — Hit bottom hand twice.

gymnastics — Move fingers in a circle around index finger.

tennis — Move wrist back and forth like swinging a tennis racquet.

swimming — Move hands in small circles.

EXERCISE

Move fists back and forth.

ice skate
Bend fingers and move hands back and forth.

roller skate
Bend two fingers and move hands back and forth.

run Hook thumb and index finger and move hands forward.

jump Bounce two fingers up and down on palm.

walk Move hands up and down like feet walking.

dance Move fingers back and forth on palm.

23

MY HOME

Move hand up cheek.

apartment Fingerspell A-P-T.

mailbox
1. Bring thumb to palm.
2. Make a box shape.

24

window Bring hands together.

door Twist hand to side.

garage Move bottom hand forward twice.

roof Touch fingertips. Move fingers away.

BEDROOM

1. Place hand on cheek.
2. Make a box shape.

bed   Place hand on cheek.

blanket   Bring hands to shoulders.

pillow
Bring hand up twice.

computer
Slide C shape up arm.

dresser
Move fists forward and down.

KITCHEN

Move K shape side to side.

refrigerator
Fingerspell R-E-F.

oven
Slide bottom hand under top hand and forward.

sink Fingerspell S-I-N-K.

microwave Open fists.

cook Move hand back and forth.

garbage can Move finger from wrist to elbow.

DINING ROOM

1. Bring hand to mouth.
2. Make a box shape.

spoon   Scoop fingers toward mouth.

fork   Slide fingers across palm.

knife   Slide top finger along bottom finger in a cutting motion.

table Tap arms together twice.

cup Make C shape and bring hand to palm.

plate Bring wrists together in a circle.

bowl Bring hands to the side.

FOOD

Touch fingers to mouth twice.

milk   Squeeze fingers together.

bread   Slide fingers across knuckles.

32

butter
Slide fingers across palm twice.

fruit
Wiggle F shape at chin.

cookie
Rotate C shape.

vegetable
Wiggle V shape at chin.

BATHROOM

Wiggle T shape.

towel   Move fists back and forth.

bathtub

1. Slide hands up chest.
2. Fingerspell T-U-B.

soap Brush fingers against palm.

comb Bend fingers. Move hand back and forth.

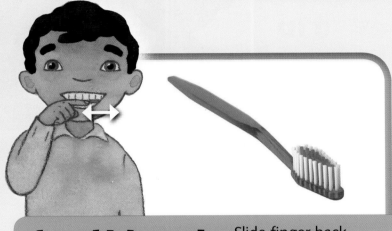

toothbrush Slide finger back and forth.

toilet Wiggle T shape.

mirror Wiggle hand in front of face.

LIVING ROOM

1. Make L shape and slide hand up chest.
2. Make a box shape.

chair Touch fingers together and tap twice.

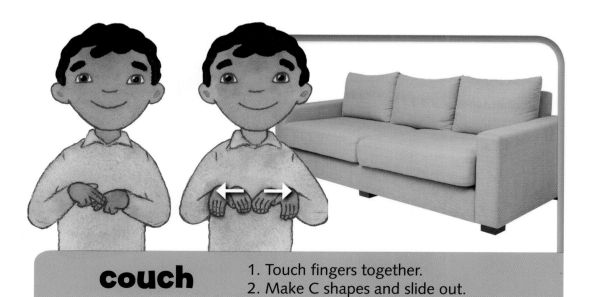

couch
1. Touch fingers together.
2. Make C shapes and slide out.

TV Fingerspell T-V.

light Open fist.

floor Slide hands to sides.

telephone Bring hand to cheek.

OUTDOORS

Tap shoulder twice.

flower   Move hand across face.

tree   Wiggle wrist back and forth.

garden   Make G shape. Move hand up arm and in a circle.

dirt Rub fingers together.

bug Put thumb on nose and bend fingers.

shovel Make digging motion.

butterfly Connect thumbs and wave hands.

BUS STOP

1. Fingerspell B-U-S.
2. Bring hand down to palm.

backpack

Tap chest twice with thumbs.

homework

1. Move hand up cheek.
2. Tap wrists together once.

bench

Slide top fingers away from body.

sit

Tap fingers once.

sign

Draw a square with fingers.

sidewalk

Move hands away from body.

CLASSROOM

1. Make C shapes and move in a circle.
2. Make a box shape.

desk Tap arms together twice.

pencil

Place finger near mouth. Slide fingers across palm.

teacher
1. Move hands away from forehead.
2. Open hands and move them down body.

crayon Wiggle fingers on chin. Pretend to draw.

paper Slide palms together twice.

map
1. Fingerspell M-A-P
2. Pretend to open map and draw a circle.

LIBRARY

Move L shape in a circle.

book Open hands like opening a book.

librarian
1. Move L shape in a circle.
2. Open hands and move them down body.

read Slide fingers across palm.

quiet Move hands away from mouth.

student
1. Make flat O shape and move hand from palm to forehead.
2. Open hands and move them down body.

PLAYGROUND

1. Make Y shapes and shake hands.
2. Move hand in a circle.

jump rope Make A shapes and move wrists in a circle.

game Make A shape and tap knuckles together twice.

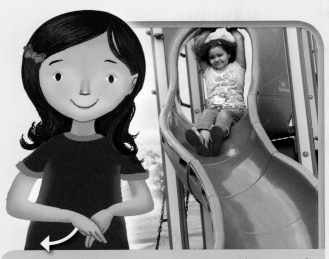

slide

Move top hand down and away from bottom hand.

swing

Move hands forward.

hopscotch

Tap fingers once then spread apart.

CAFETERIA

Make C shape and touch both corners of chin.

tray Move wrists forward.

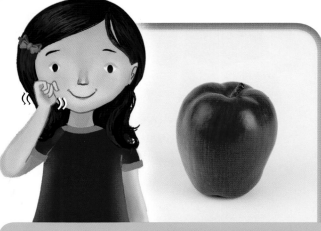

apple Wiggle X shape at corner of mouth.

loud 1. Point to ear. 2. Shake fists.

sandwich Bring hand in between thumb and pointer finger.

hungry Make C shape and move hand down chest.

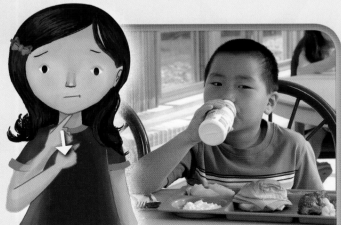

thirsty Point to chin and move finger down throat.

SUBJECTS

Bend fingers.

math Make M shapes and cross.

science Make A shapes. Circle hands near chest but not touching.

history Make H shape and shake fingers twice.

art Wiggle pinky down palm.

music Move hand back and forth along arm.

English Grab bottom hand and move toward body.

COLORS

Wiggle fingers at chin.

red — Touch lips and curl finger.

yellow — Twist Y shape.

blue — Twist B shape.

green — Twist G shape.

orange Squeeze fingers together twice.

purple Twist P shape.

black Move finger across forehead.

white Move hand away from chest and bring fingers together.

pink Make P shape and slide down lips twice.

SHAPES

Make A shapes and wiggle hands down body.

circle   Draw a circle with finger.

rectangle   Draw a rectangle with fingers.

square   Draw a square with fingers.

triangle   Draw a triangle with fingers.

heart   Draw a heart on chest.

star   Slide fingers back and forth.

NUMBERS

Touch fingertips twice
while twisting wrists.

0

1

2

3

4

5

6

7

8

9

10

100

PEOPLE

1. Make P shapes.
2. Move hands in circles.

man   Bring hand to chest.

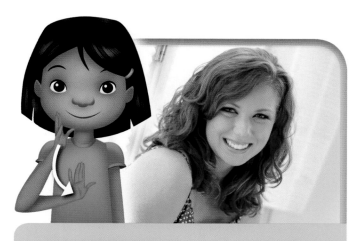

woman   Bring hand to chest.

you Point to person.

me Point to self.

boy Close hand while moving it away from forehead.

girl Slide thumb down cheek.

COMMUNITY HELPERS

Place fist on palm and move hands up.

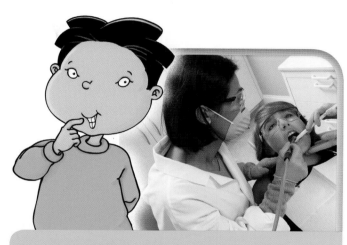

dentist Bring finger to mouth.

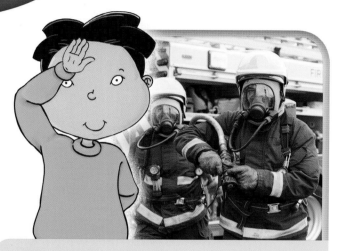

firefighter Tap forehead twice.

paramedic
1. Make a cross on arm.
2. Open hands and move them down body.

police officer

Make C shape and tap chest twice.

veterinarian

Fingerspell V-E-T.

mail carrier

1. Bring thumb to palm.
2. Open hands and move them down body.

AT THE STORE

Make flat O shapes and move fingers up.

shopping/buy
Move top hand away from palm.

money
Bring hand to palm.

dollar
Slide fingers along top of other hand and into a fist.

penny
Point to forehead and move hand away.

quarter 1. Point to forehead. 2. Wiggle middle finger.

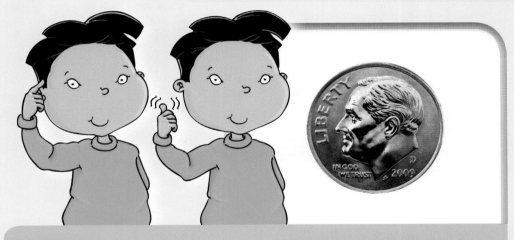

dime 1. Point to forehead. 2. Make a fist and wiggle thumb.

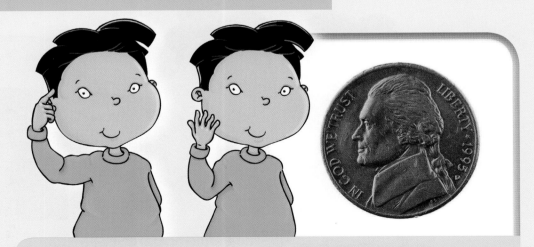

nickel 1. Point to forehead. 2. Hold up 5 fingers.

ON THE FARM

Slide thumb across chin.

tractor Make T shapes and move hands as if driving a tractor.

sheep Open and close fingers like scissors while moving hand up arm.

farmer
1. Slide thumb across chin.
2. Open hands and move them down body.

pig Put hand on chin and move fingers up and down.

horse Bend first two fingers.

barn Fingerspell B-A-R-N.

chicken Open and close fingers.

cow Make Y shape and wiggle pinky.

AT A RESTAURANT

Make R shape and touch both sides of chin.

menu
1. Move hand down palm twice.
2. Open hands like opening a book.

server
1. Move hands forward.
2. Open hands and move them down body.

salt Wiggle fingers.

pepper Make F shape and shake hand twice.

eat Bring fingers to mouth.

chef
1. Move hand back and forth.
2. Open hands and move them down body.

AT THE DOCTOR'S OFFICE

1. Make D shape and bring hand to wrist.
2. Make O shapes and cross hands.

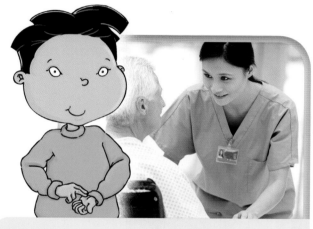

nurse Place two fingers on wrist.

sick Wiggle middle fingers on forehead and stomach.

shot Point finger and touch arm.

bandage
Slide two fingers across back of hand.

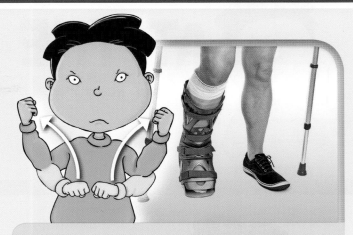

broken
Move fists up and away from each other.

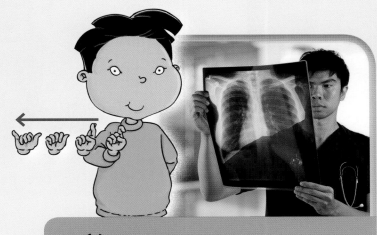

X-ray
Fingerspell X-R-A-Y.

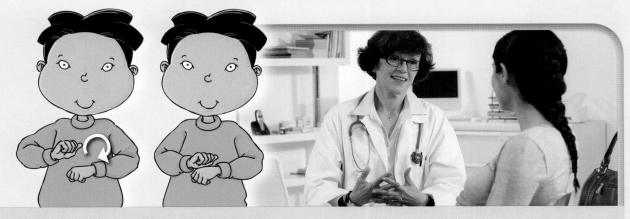

appointment
1. Make A shapes and move top hand in a circle.
2. Place on other hand.

AT THE ZOO

Fingerspell Z-O-O.

elephant — Move hand down and away from nose.

lion — Curve hand and slide over head.

giraffe — Make G shape and move up neck.

penguin — Place hands at hips and waddle.

alligator Open and close curved hands.

shark Place hand on top of head like a fin.

monkey Scratch sides twice.

bear Cross hands and scratch chest twice.

zebra Bend fingers and make stripes on chest.

AT THE CARNIVAL

Bend fingers and move in small circles.

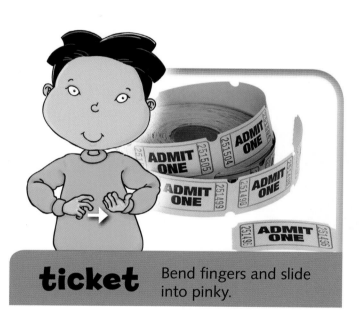

ticket
Bend fingers and slide into pinky.

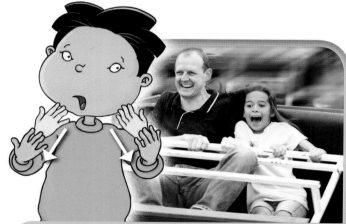

scream
Curl hands and move away from mouth.

cotton candy
Twist finger at corner of mouth.

roller coaster

Move hand up and down.

haunted house

1. Shake hands.
2. Touch fingertips and move hands down.

popcorn

1. Make fists.
2. Point one finger at a time, back and forth.

AT THE BEACH

Move hands up and down like waves.

water Make W shape and tap mouth twice.

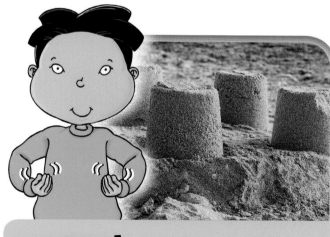

sand Rub fingers together.

whistle Bring two fingers to mouth.

sunglasses

1. Open fist.
2. Close fingers at side of face.

swimsuit

1. Move hands in small circles.
2. Slide hands along chest and waist.

lifeguard

1. Make L shapes and move up chest.
2. Cross hands and make G shapes.

TRANSPORTATION

Move fist forward and back.

car   Move hands as if driving a car.

bus   Fingerspell B-U-S.

truck   Fingerspell T-R-U-C-K.

bicycle
Move hands in circles like the pedals of a bike.

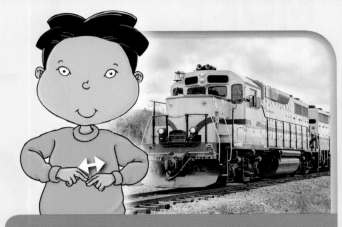

train
Slide fingers back and forth.

boat
Cup hands and move forward.

airplane
Point thumb, index, and pinky fingers. Move hand forward.

street
Move hands forward.

MORE PLACES TO VISIT

bank   Fingerspell B-A-N-K.

park   Fingerspell P-A-R-K.

hospital

Draw a cross on shoulder.

mall

Fingerspell M-A-L-L.

movie theater

Move hand
back and forth.

grocery store

1. Bring fingers to mouth.
2. Move fingers forward twice.

hair salon

1. Make cutting sign.
2. Open hands and move them down body.

gas station

1. Bring thumb into fist.
2. Move fingers forward twice.

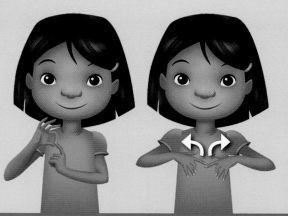

SPECIAL EVENTS

1. Grab finger and pull up.
2. Bend middle fingers. Curve up and out.

party   Make P shapes and twist wrists.

celebration   Make X shapes and move wrists in small circles.

wedding Grab fingers with other hand.

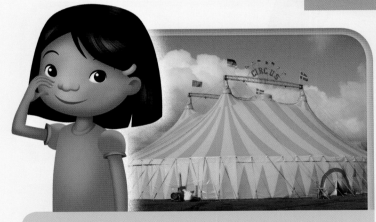

circus Close fingers and wiggle hand in front of nose.

applause Twist hands near face.

HOLIDAYS

Tap chest twice.

New Year's Day

1. Slide back of hand over palm.
2. Make S shape. Move top hand in a circle.
3. Bring arm down to other arm.

Valentine's Day

1. Make a heart shape on chest.
2. Bring arm down to other arm.

Halloween

Cover face and then open hands, like playing peek-a-boo.

Thanksgiving

Move hands away from mouth with a small bounce.

Christmas

Make C shape and move across chest.

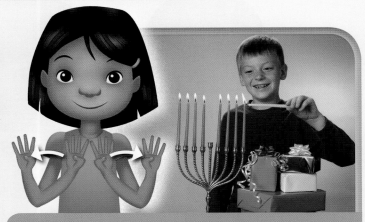

Hanukkah

Hold up four fingers. Slide hands to the side.

BIRTHDAY

Bring middle finger from chin to chest.

friend 1. Lock fingers. 2. Repeat with other hand on top.

balloon Move hands into a circle, like blowing up a balloon.

candy Twist finger on cheek.

candles Wiggle fingers and point to wrist.

ice cream Make S shape and move down twice in front of mouth.

gift Make X shapes and move forward twice.

cake Make C shape and slide down hand.

TELLING TIME

Tap wrist twice.

morning Move hand up and toward body.

afternoon Move hand away from body.

night Move hand down and away from body.

week Point finger and move hand across palm.

Monday
Tuesday
Wednesday
Thursday
Friday
Saturday
Sunday

month Point finger and slide down hand.

year Make S shapes and move top hand in a circle.

minute Point finger and move wrist forward quickly.

hour Point finger and move hand in a circle.

DAYS OF THE WEEK

Point finger and move hand across palm.

Monday

Make M shape and move hand in a circle.

Tuesday

Make T shape and move hand in a circle.

Wednesday

Make W shape and move hand in a circle.

Thursday

Make H shape and move
hand in a circle.

Friday

Make F shape and move
hand in a circle.

Saturday

Make S shape and move
hand in a circle.

Sunday

Move palms down.

MONTHS

Point finger and slide down hand.

January
Fingerspell J-A-N.

February
Fingerspell F-E-B.

March
Fingerspell M-A-R-C-H.

April

Fingerspell A-P-R-I-L.

May

Fingerspell M-A-Y.

June

Fingerspell J-U-N-E.

July

Fingerspell J-U-L-Y.

August

Fingerspell A-U-G.

September

Fingerspell S-E-P-T.

October

Fingerspell O-C-T.

November

Fingerspell N-O-V.

December

Fingerspell D-E-C.

SEASONS

1. Make S shape.
2. Move fist in a circle against palm.

rain   Move hands down.

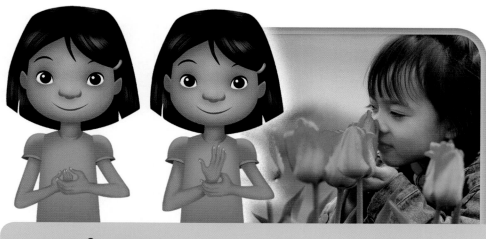

spring   Move hand up and through other hand twice.

autumn Move hand past elbow twice, like a leaf falling from a tree.

winter Shake fists as if shivering.

snow Wiggle fingers while bringing hands down.

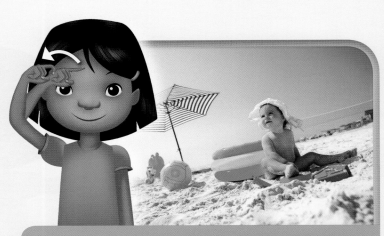

summer Bend finger while sliding across forehead.

GREETINGS

Move hand away from forehead.

hello Wave hand.

good-bye Open and close hand.

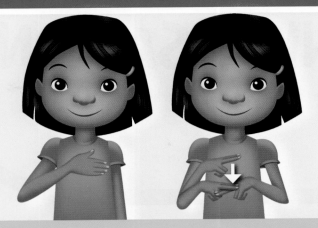

My name is _____
1. Palm to chest. 2. Bring fingers together. 3. Fingerspell name.

What's your name?
1. Point to person. 2. Bring fingers together. 3. Move hands in small circles.

Nice to meet you
1. Slide palm across other palm. 2. Bring wrists together. 3. Point to person.

CONVERSATION

Make C shapes and move hands back and forth.

yes Make a fist. Move hand up and down.

no Bring fingers together.

maybe
1. Raise one hand while lowering the other.
2. Move hands back and forth.

more Bring fingers together.

now Make Y shapes and bring hands down.

later Make L shape and move wrist forward.

or

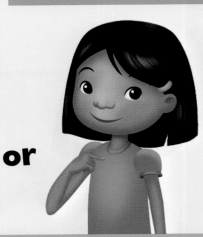

Combine the shapes I, L, and Y.

I love you

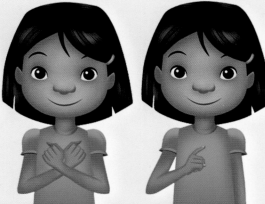

1. Point to self. 2. Cross wrists. 3. Point to person.

QUESTIONS

Draw a question mark with finger.

who Touch thumb to chin and wiggle index finger

what Shake hands slightly.

when Circle index finger around other finger.

where Wiggle finger twice.

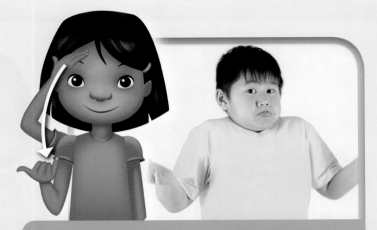

why
1. Touch fingers to forehead.
2. Bring hand down and make Y shape.

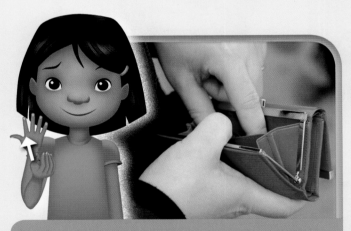

how much Open hand with palm facing up.

how many Open hands with palms facing up.

MANNERS

Touch chest twice with thumb.

please Make a circle on chest.

thank you Move hand away from lips.

excuse me Slide fingers along palm.

congratulations Clasp hands together and shake twice.

I'm sorry Make a fist and move hand in a circle.

OPPOSITES

Move fingers apart.

big Make L shapes and move hands apart.

small Bring hands close together.

good Move hand away from mouth.

bad Move hand away from mouth while turning palm down.

new Slide back of hand over palm.

old Close fist while moving hand down.

fast Bend fingers as you move hands up.

slow Slide hand up along arm.

hot Make C shape and move hand away from mouth and down.

cold Shake fists as if shivering.

INDEX

A+ Books are published by Capstone Press,
1710 Roe Crest Drive, North Mankato, Minnesota 56003
www.capstoneyoungreaders.com

Library of Congress Cataloging-in-Publication Data
Clay, Kathryn.
Time to sign: sign language for kids / by Kathryn Clay; illustrated by Michael Reid, Randy Chewning,
 Margeaux Lucas, and Daniel Griffo.
 pages cm
 Includes index.
 Audience: Grade K to 3.
 ISBN 978-1-62065-687-7 (paperback)
1. American Sign Language—Juvenile literature. 2. Sign language—Juvenile literature.
I. Reid, Michael, 1958– illustrator. II. Title.
HV2476.C563 2014
419'.7—dc23   2013021191

Editorial Credits
Tracy Davies McCabe, designer; Svetlana Zhurkin, media researcher;
Kathy McColley, production specialist

Content Consultant
Kari Sween, adjunct instructor of American Sign Language,
Minnesota State University, Mankato

Photo Credits
Capstone Studio: Karon Dubke, 8, 9 (top left, middle, bottom right), 10 (bottom right), 11 (top left, bottom left), 12 (top), 13
(middle, bottom), 16 (top right), 17 (top, bottom left), 18 (top), 19 (top left, bottom right), 25, 26 (top), 27 (top, middle), 28
(bottom), 29 (top), 30 (top right), 31 (bottom right), 32 (bottom), 33 (top left, bottom left), 34 (top), 35 (bottom left), 38 (left,
bottom right), 39, 41 (bottom left), 42, 43, 44, 45 (top, bottom), 46, 47, 48, 49 (top, bottom), 50 (bottom left), 51, 84 (top), 86
(bottom), 87 (bottom right), 88, 89, 90 (top left), 99 (top right); Dreamstime, 22 (bottom), 63 (bottom), 74 (bottom), 79 (top
left); iStockphotos, 5, 6, 7, 20 (bottom right), 21 (top left), 63 (top), 69 (bottom), 80 (top), 83 (bottom), 85 (middle, bottom);
Shutterstock, cover, 9 (top right, bottom left), 10 (left, top right), 11 (top right, middle, bottom right), 12 (bottom), 13
(top), 14, 15, 16 (left, bottom right), 17 (middle, bottom right), 18 (bottom), 19 (top right, middle, bottom left), 20 (left,
top right), 21 (top right, middle, bottom), 22 (top), 23, 24, 26 (bottom), 27 (bottom), 28 (top), 29 (bottom), 30 (left,
bottom right), 31 (top, bottom left), 32 (top), 33 (top right, bottom right), 34 (bottom), 35 (top, middle, bottom
right), 36, 37, 38 (top right), 40, 41 (top, bottom right), 45 (middle), 49 (middle), 50 (top, bottom right), 60, 61, 62,
63 (middle), 64, 65, 66, 67, 68, 69 (top, middle), 70, 71, 72, 73 (top, bottom), 74 (top), 75, 76, 77, 78, 79 (top right,
middle, bottom), 80 (bottom), 81, 82, 83 (top), 84 (bottom), 85 (top), 86 (top), 87 (top, middle, bottom left), 90
(top right, bottom), 91, 94, 95, 96, 97, 98, 99 (top left, bottom), 100, 101, 104, 105, 106, 107, 108, 109; Svetlana
Zhurkin, 73 (middle)

Note to Parents, Teachers, and Librarians
This accessible, visual guide uses full color photographs and illustrations and inviting content
to introduce young readers to American Sign Language. The book provides an early
introduction to reference materials and encourages further learning by including the
following sections: Table of Contents, Alphabet Chart, and Index.

For Madelyn —K.C.

Printed in the United States of America in North Mankato, Minnesota.
112015   009334R